Happy Christm

Love, Us

2012

C000228369

IMAGES
of America

VINTAGE TAMPA
STOREFRONTS AND SCENES

Best Wishes
John V. Crickett

Pictured here in 1956 is Tampa's beloved S.H. Kress Variety Store towering over the shoppers on Franklin Street like a queen to her subjects. The four-story structure located at 811 North Franklin Street was designed with an elaborate facade featuring Renaissance Revival terra-cotta ornamentations, considered by many to be the most beautiful building in all of downtown Tampa. Constructed in 1929, this was one of Tampa's most popular dime stores for over 50 years. The S.H. Kress Company's team of architects did not follow a blueprint for their chain of stores; rather, the company designed each store with its own unique character to stand out on a city's main street. The building was designated a National Historic Landmark in 1983 and still stands today. (John V. Cinchett.)

ON THE COVER: In this scene from 1956, the southeast corner of Franklin and Twiggs Streets is captured, and it is a busy day in downtown Tampa. The billboard on the rooftop advertises the College Shop Menswear store, one of the stores in the building below. On the corner is the well-known Downtown Cigar Store, featuring Hav-A-Tampa cigars and proudly announcing on the sign, "The finest cigars in the world are made in Tampa." Looking south along Franklin Street are many of Tampa's family-owned shops, including the Schwobilt Menswear Store, the Diana Super Outlet clothing store, the Darling Shops Department Store, and Jack Pendola's Menswear store. (HCPLC.)

IMAGES
of America

Vintage Tampa
Storefronts and Scenes

John V. Cinchett

ARCADIA
PUBLISHING

Published by Arcadia Publishing
Charleston, South Carolina

Printed in the United States of America

Library of Congress Control Number: 2011942689

For all general information, please contact Arcadia Publishing:
Telephone 843-853-2070
Fax 843-853-0044
E-mail sales@arcadiapublishing.com
For customer service and orders:
Toll-Free 1-888-313-2665

Visit us on the Internet at www.arcadiapublishing.com

This book is dedicated to my father, John F. Cinchett, and grandfather Frank Cinchett—Tampa's legendary neon sign kings. Their virtues in life were simple: a hardworking ethic and selfless dedication to the family that still serves to inspire generations today. Heaven certainly must be a brighter place with these men lighting up every cloud with one of their famous neon creations.

Here is the Alpine Liquor Store, Tampa's oldest family-owned liquor store, pictured in 1940. When Al Manolt Sr. opened his store in 1936, he decided to offer something never before seen in Tampa—cocktail curb service. The customer could drive up and have their cocktail order taken at curbside from the bartender, who would then bring the drink outside to the patron for enjoyment inside their car. Located at 7501 Nebraska Avenue in Seminole Heights, the store has been operated by four generations of the Manolt family. (John V. Cinchett.)

CONTENTS

ACKNOWLEDGMENTS

The author first and foremost must thank the gracious residents of Tampa who welcomed me into their homes to interview them about the history of their family businesses and collect their historic pictures. I am very appreciative of the many nostalgic Tampa residents and civic leaders who believe in the importance of preserving our rich history.

Several photographs appearing in this publication are selected from the Cinchett Collection, which is a valuable archive of Tampa photographs and film reels taken by the Cinchett family between 1949 and 1969 for their neon sign company (Cinchett Neon Signs, Inc.) that operated in Tampa from 1947 to 1997. That collection was featured in another Arcadia Publishing pictorial titled *Vintage Tampa Signs and Scenes*.

My sincerest appreciation to the University of South Florida Special Collections Library and librarian Andy Huse for their assistance with several photographs appearing here from the historic Robertson-Fresh Collection. Those images will include the acknowledgment (USFSCL). The author wishes to acknowledge the Tampa-Hillsborough County Public Library for their assistance with several images from the Burgert Brothers Collection, and those images will include the acknowledgment (HCPLC). These two library staffs are to be highly commended for their continued dedication to the preservation and promotion of historic Tampa photographs.

Patrick and Angie Manteiga, the owners of *La Gaceta* newspaper, are graciously acknowledged for their kind assistance with several historic photographs and are to be recognized for their continued support of historic preservation efforts. My most grateful appreciation is awarded to the *Penny Saver News* with special thanks to Sulphur Springs historian Linda Hope and editor Gail Hope for their assistance with researching several historic photographs and for their passionate dedication to historic preservation.

All other photographs appearing herein are from the private collection of author John V. Cinchett and may not be photocopied, posted online, or reproduced without exclusive permission from the author.

The author wishes to offer sincerest gratitude to several individuals for their kind assistance with photographic restoration work: Sam Sellers and Golden Triangle Photography, Bob Baggett Photography, and Dan Perez, webmaster for the www.Tampapix.com website, which is dedicated to the preservation of historic Tampa photographs.

I also want to congratulate Mario Nunez and Steve Cannella, the creators of the *Tampa Natives Show*, for their historic preservation efforts in continuing to document the rich heritage of Tampa through interviews with longtime residents and civic leaders.

INTRODUCTION

One of the fondest childhood memories harkens back to those Saturday-morning shopping trips downtown with mom or grandma. Shopping was an adventure to a magical place and a welcome relief from those day-to-day activities. Planning a trip downtown was an event not taken lightly; ladies would dress up in their best Sunday dresses, and gentlemen would don suits and ties. How exciting it was to spend the day shopping for that new pair of gloves or a new hat for dad. Maybe it was a trip to the toy shop for a reward from a good report card or for helping dad clean out the garage. Friends would often gather at the corner drugstore soda fountain for an ice cream sundae and then make plans to take in a show at one of downtown's many movie houses. Many Tampa residents discovered air-conditioning for the first time in downtown's department stores and theaters. It was not uncommon for children to ride their neighborhood streetcar to downtown Tampa with $1 in their pocket for the whole day—that would get a trolley ride, a movie ticket, popcorn, and soda and have enough left over for a hamburger from the Woolworth's lunch counter on the way home.

Longtime Tampa residents fondly recall Tampa's glory years. From the 1940s through the 1960s, downtown Tampa was a thriving, bustling hub of the city's shopping and business district, both day and night. Flashing, colorful neon signs lit up every block calling out to throngs of shoppers. It was during this period that downtown Tampa was the center of all activity. Before the arrival of shopping centers and malls, the sidewalks of downtown were lined with all types of stores and shops. Most neighborhoods around the city would have some small, family-owned stores and shops that residents could walk over to, but everyone would head to downtown Tampa for regular shopping trips. Ladies of Tampa would stroll past their favorite dress shops, like Viola Todd's or Poller's. Gentlemen found their way to popular shirt shops, like Wolf Brothers or Jensen's. Of course, downtown also was brimming with department store favorites like Maas Brothers, Haber's, Grant's, O'Falk's, Kress, and Newberry's. Life in Tampa revolved around the downtown scene for every type of business from tailors to lawyers and from realtors to roofers. During downtown's heyday, some of the most interesting sights were the elaborate window dressings found in the many department stores lining downtown's sidewalks. The larger department stores all employed staff to create vivid, colorful scenes using the store merchandise to attract shoppers. Storefront windows became the showplace for all the latest fashion trends, redesigned appliances, and popular home furnishings of the day.

Long before corporate America made its way into downtown Tampa's skyscrapers, the city's commercial infrastructure was based on the success of longtime, well-established, family-owned businesses for every type of industry: from print shops and dress shops to appliance stores and loan companies. They all found success along Tampa's expanding highways of the 1940s, 1950s, and 1960s. Family-owned businesses thrived on Tampa's postwar growth. In every neighborhood, savvy, young entrepreneurs made their dreams become a reality in brick and mortar. Hardworking families with a vision for their future devoted their lives to businesses of every type. Many of these stores would see three and four generations of family ownership of those proudly carrying on their family's Tampa heritage. Businesses included neighborhood markets, hardware stores, furniture shops, drugstores, bakeries, toy stores, paint stores, bicycle shops, and the list goes on and on. Local residents enjoyed the personal attention and friendly service offered there and would always return for shopping trips. These family-owned places became the backbone of Tampa's industrial success, thriving on the population boom of the 1950s and highway expansions of the 1960s.

These extraordinary vintage photographs will bring back those happy memories of simpler times and pleasant days. In these pictures are many historic treasures to discover with many iconic signs and symbols from ages past. Each picture presents a rare look into Tampa's historic past and serves as a photographic testament to the hardworking ethic of the Tampa business community. Every photograph tells a very special story. Take a moment now to stroll back in time to Tampa's glory years.

Here is an incredible glimmering nighttime scene of downtown Tampa from 1956. This photograph captures the sparkling neon signs along Tampa's central shopping district on Franklin Street between Madison and Twiggs Streets looking northwest. Many of the city's most popular stores can be seen here. Starting from the left and continuing clockwise are Magnon Jewelers, Fremacs Menswear, Madison Drugs, Stein's Clothing, Duval Jewelers, Mangel's Department Store, Maas Brothers, Wolf Brothers, O'Falks Department Store, and the Super Outlet Store's neon sign, which is just visible on the right. The car in the foreground is a brand-new 1956 Ford Custom sedan. (Hector Colado.)

One

DOWNTOWN AND
HYDE PARK

This 1952 scene captures another busy shopping day in downtown Tampa. This view is looking south on Franklin Street near the intersection of Polk Street in front of Woolworth's, Tampa's favorite dime store. At right is O'Falk's, another favorite department store. Before the arrival of discount stores, cities and towns across the country were dotted with variety stores—larger, modern versions of 19th-century general stores. The stores were fittingly known as "5-and-10s" because most of their wares were near those pricing points. These dime stores commonly found their ways in the downtown shopping districts, and all of them shared some common aesthetics, including similar storefront signage and store layouts. Even the names followed a recognizable pattern, such as F.W. Woolworth's, J.J. Newberry, W.T. Grant's, and S.H. Kress.

Here is the Grayson's Department Store at 909 North Franklin Street in 1946, which specialized in fine ladies' clothing. The storefront windows are decorated for the latest in fall fashions of the 1940s with ladies' fine dresses, lingerie, handbags, shoes, hats, and gloves. The tile work at the entrance is designed to incorporate the name of the store—a clever way to ensure that shoppers walking by would see the store name as they made their way along the sidewalk. (HCPLC.)

In this 1952 photograph, the Franklin Street shopping district has been captured looking south from Polk Street. At left are many popular downtown destinations, including Butler's Shoes, the Tampa Theatre, Lerner's Dress Shop, Chandler's Shoes, and Haber's Department Store. On the right are Maas Brothers, Wolf Brothers, and the Florida Theatre. (HCPLC.)

This nostalgic 1958 scene captures the 600 block of Florida Avenue looking north between Twiggs and Zack Streets. Among the businesses are the W.H. Wells Realty Company, Tampa Stamp & Coin Exchange, Florida Shoe Hospital, a stationery and gift shop, Fulghum's Office Furniture, and the Family Finance Service. All of these businesses were family owned.

Pictured in 1950 is the popular Butler's Shoe Store at 713 North Franklin Street in the Tampa Theatre building. The storefront entrance is an elaborate display of Broadway-style neon and flashing lights. Advertised prices are new ladies' shoes for $2.99 and $3.99. Ladies stockings are advertised at two for $1.

The Hayman Jewelry Company started in an unusual place—the trunk of a Ford Model T. In 1932, Solomon Hayman was trying to get into the jewelry business during hard times, so he asked his doctor for a $500 loan and began selling watches out of the trunk of his car. A year later, the Hayman Jewelry Company store was established in downtown Tampa and in 1947 moved to the corner of Cass and Franklin Streets, as pictured above in 1968. During the 1950s, the store became one of Tampa's most popular. In the 1950 photograph below, S.L. Hayman is seated at his office surrounded by some of the other products sold in the store, including radios and appliances. The third-generation family-operated store is now at 305 Madison Street and is the last downtown jewelry store of that era still standing.

Here is the Hayman Jewelry Company's appliance store at 215 Cass Street in 1956. The store featured Hotpoint appliances, and in the storefront windows are several of the latest models, including an industrial four-burner coffee maker on sale for $74. Among the other items on display are several vintage table radios. The 1956 photograph below shows the interior of the store on the corner of Franklin and Cass Streets. Pictured at left is S.L. Hayman with employee Betty Wichen. Also in the rear of the store are employees Mary Alla Fuentes and a young Arthur Yates, the store watch repairman who later would open his own successful South Tampa jewelry store.

This 1957 photograph captures a busy scene in front of Bakers Shoes at 701 North Franklin Street. A large gathering of ladies is window shopping. The storefront windows are advertising new ladies' shoes on sale from $3.99 to $4.99, and ladies' gloves are 79¢.

This amazing photograph captures Lamar Jewelers at 515 Tampa Street in 1955. The elaborate neon signs are actually taller than the entire storefront. Of note is the vintage clock above the entrance. Having a storefront clock was a popular trend during this era and a clever way to have pedestrians notice the name of the business when they checked the time. During the 1940s and 1950s, neon signs dominated the streets of downtown Tampa on storefronts and rooftops. These were the glory years for neon signs, and they became an iconic symbol of the 1950s. (USFSCL.)

ADAMS JEWELRY CO.

This jewelry store certainly must have been the most elegant of all those downtown. The Adams Jewelry Company was located at 609 Franklin Street in this 1940 image. Fringed drapery frames the entire storefront window, surrounding a lovely display of necklaces, jeweled purses, jewelry boxes, and clocks.

Shoppers could purchase a brand-new pair of ladies' shoes here for $2.99, as advertised in the storefront window. The latest shoe fashions from 1942 for men are also on sale, priced at $1.99 per pair at Roger's Smart Shoes, located at 911 Franklin Street. Before the arrival of shopping centers and malls, shoppers made their way to downtown Tampa where the streets were lined with shoe stores, dress shops, and clothing stores. Of note is the elaborate Broadway-style neon signage that stretches across the entire storefront. (USFSCL.)

The Haubenstock family has a long history in Tampa's furniture market. In 1939, Saul Haubenstock established the Southern Furniture Company (pictured above in 1941) at 1110 Florida Avenue, specializing in high-quality used furniture and antiques he had shipped by railcar from auction houses in New York City. Saul had operated several furniture stores in Manhattan during the 1930s but saw great potential in the Tampa market and was lured here by the welcoming climate. Their store delivery vehicle was Saul's 1938 LaSalle sedan. In the scene below from 1956, employees have gathered in front of the store for a company photograph; seated is company founder Saul Haubenstock. The family operated for nearly 30 years in this landmark building, which still stands today.

This 1940 scene captures the Southern Furniture Company at 1110 Florida Avenue, and standing out front are, from left to right, Alfred Haubenstock, Saul Haubenstock, and Howard Haubenstock. During the 1940s, the store was awarded the contract to refinish the furniture at MacDill Air Force Base. In a unique alliance with Elkes Pontiac Co. across the street from the store, they used the dealership's automobile paint-drying ovens to bake on the new finish for desks and chairs. In 1967, the Haubenstock family established Tampa's first Ethan Allen furniture store, pictured below shortly after its opening at 6200 North Dale Mabry Highway. The store was the first of its kind with a layout that featured a fully furnished model of each room in the home. Three generations of the Haubenstock family have continued their tradition of service in the Tampa furniture store industry.

Pictured in 1952 is Liggett's Rexall Drugs, located at the southeast corner of Franklin and Zack Streets. This was one of downtown Tampa's largest and most popular drugstores for many years. The scene is certainly a busy one outside the store with shoppers strolling along Franklin Street. The scene below from 1948 captures several shoppers inside Liggett's, including some soldiers who appear to be more interested in the young lady behind the counter than what is on display in it.

Haber's Department Store at 613 North Franklin Street is pictured in 1956. Haber's was one of Tampa's most popular family-owned department stores from the 1930s through the 1960s. In the storefront windows are the latest in ladies' fashions of the 1950s. The 1951 city directory listed Leon A. Haber as president and Albert Haber as secretary. Al Haber became a well-known Tampa businessman and socialite, moving up the corporate ladder in the family's department store business. In 1975, the Habers' legacy came to an end with the death of Al Haber, and the subsequent investigation became one of Tampa's most notorious murder cases in history, making headlines with a complex story of plots and twists involving the department store mogul's wife.

Here is Mangel's, one of Tampa's favorite department stores for ladies, pictured in 1952 at 606 North Franklin Street. Mangel's was an exclusive ladies' wear store offering dresses, hats, gloves, scarves, handbags, bathing suits, and lingerie. They also sold children's clothing. When this photograph was taken, the store was operated by Joe Barchan, Emanuel Gottfried, and Virginia Messina.

Here are two of Tampa's most iconic storefronts from the 1940s. Pictured above in 1946 is the Cabana Club Soda Shop at Vernor's Ginger Ale Company, which was located at 211 East Platt Street in downtown Tampa. The most distinguishing feature of the storefront was the giant animated neon sign that captivated motorists driving by with two elves rocking back and forth on a seesaw. Pictured below in 1951 is the Old Fort Sandwich Shop and Liquor Store at 301 South Franklin Street. The building was designed to replicate old Fort Brooke, which is the original establishment that eventually became the city of Tampa. (Both, HCPLC.)

This 1940 scene along the 600 block of Franklin Street captures several stores and shops along the east side of the shopping district. From left to right appear the Schwob Company menswear store, Haber's ladies' clothing store, and Adams Jewelry Company. In later years, Haber's expanded into a larger department store. The sign for Haber's reads, "Ladies Snappy Clothes." (USFSCL.)

This bustling downtown corner scene captures Tampa's J.C. Penney's Department Store in 1950 at the northwest corner of Franklin and Polk Streets. All of the large, nationally recognized department stores were located downtown during this era. In the building next door is the popular Goff Jewelry Company. (HCPLC.)

The legendary Tampa success story of Maas Brothers begins in 1886 with the opening of their first general store at the corner of Franklin and Twiggs Streets. Called the Dry Goods Palace, it was a small storefront in the J.C. Field building that occupied that corner. The young Abraham Maas and his brother Isaac were already well established in the dry goods business, starting out in Macon and Savannah, Georgia. But they wanted to move into an area that could promise them a bright future, so they chose Tampa and opened their first store in December 1886. In 1920, after continued success and growth of their business, the brothers proudly purchased the American Bank building located at the southwest corner of Franklin and Zack Streets (pictured here in 1952 with the trademark Maas Brothers sign). The new store officially opened in October 1921. (HCPLC.)

This rare image from 1952 captures shoppers inside the Maas Brothers Department Store, and what a busy day it must have been. In the domestics department, a large crowd of well-dressed Tampa ladies are selecting linens, curtains, towels, and fabrics. The scene below from 1957 captures the Maas Brothers toy department. On display is a vintage collection of 1950s favorites for children, including dolls, bicycles, stuffed animals, friction cars, swings, slides, dollhouses, and board games. Maas Brothers Department Store was an institution in downtown Tampa for more than 70 years and a local favorite that longtime Tampa residents still fondly remember today. (Both, USFSCL.)

Here is the entrance to Woolworth's at the corner of Franklin and Polk Streets in 1948. In the storefront window to the left is an assortment of toy tanks and cars. There is an advertisement for chicken club sandwiches for 40¢ at the luncheonette. The small sign at right says, "Visit our bakery department—everything baked daily." The scene below from 1950 captures the store interior, and to the right is the famous Woolworth's luncheonette. The world is a sadder place without Woolworth's. Along Woolworth's aisles was just about anything that might appear on a shopping list. Entering Woolworth's made a dull day come alive. There was something for everyone, from dishes to hardware, cosmetics to candy, and tools to toys. There was even a pet department. (Both, USFSCL.)

F. W. Woolworth Co.

BACON and TOMATO . . . . 50¢
Toasted Three Decker Sandwich

BAKED HAM and CHEESE . . . . 60¢
Toasted Three Decker Sandwich

CHICKEN SALAD . . . . 65¢
Toasted Three Decker Sandwich

HAM SALAD and EGG SALAD . . . . . 50¢
Toasted Three Decker Sandwich
Above available on two slices of bread on request.

PLAIN or TOASTED SANDWICHES

HAM SALAD Sandwich . . . . 30¢

EGG SALAD Sandwich . . . . 30¢

AMERICAN CHEESE Sandwich . . . . . . 30¢

PRESSED HAM Sandwich . . . . 30¢

FOR A REAL TREAT!
TRY OUR SUPER DE-LUXE HAM SANDWICH – BAKED HAM SLICED VERY THIN AND STACKED
HIGH ON PLAIN BREAD, TOAST OR HARD ROLL
40¢   YOU WILL LIKE IT!   40¢

Fountain Features

DE LUXE
TULIP SUNDAE 25¢
2 Dippers of Ice Cream covered
with Crushed Fruit or
Fresh Fruits in Season

CHOICE OF
STRAWBERRY, PINEAPPLE, CHERRY,
CHOCOLATE OR HOT FUDGE
Topped with Whipped Topping
Roasted Nuts and Cherry Ring

SUPER JUMBO
BANANA SPLIT 39¢
½ Banana covered with 3
Dippers of Ice Cream and
Crushed Fruits or Fresh Fruits
in Season

CHOICE OF
STRAWBERRY, PINEAPPLE, CHERRY,
CHOCOLATE OR HOT FUDGE
Topped with Whipped Topping
and Roasted Nuts

EXTRA RICH
ICE CREAM SODA 25¢

POPULAR FLAVORS

Made with 2 Dippers of Ice Cream
Crushed Fruit or Fresh Fruits
in Season

MALTED MILK . . . . 25¢
Popular FLAVORS   Made with 2 Dippers of Ice Cream

MILK SHAKE . . . . 25¢
Popular FLAVORS   Made with 2 Dippers of Ice Cream

BANANA SPLIT Regular . . . . 25¢
Popular FLAVORS   Made with 3 Dippers of Ice Cream

FRESH ORANGE JUICE . . . . Regular 20¢   Large 30¢
Freshly Squeezed to Order

DRINK
Coca-Cola
KING SIZE 10¢

HOT NESTLE'S WITH WHIPPED TOPPING . . . . . 15¢
AND WAFERS

APPLE PIE . . . . Per Cut 15¢
10¢ Additional with Ice Cream

Home Style Desserts   **LAYER CAKE** . . . . Per Cut 15¢
10¢ Additional with Ice Cream

WOOLWORTH COFFEE — ALWAYS GOOD

HAVE A COKE   **Coca-Cola**   GOES GOOD WITH FOOD

NO. 3454 REV. 9-60

Here is the menu at the Woolworth's luncheonette from 1960. Among the advertised prices are sandwiches for 30¢, Coca-Cola for 10¢, banana splits for 25¢, milk shakes for 25¢, and slices of apple pie for 15¢. During the 1940s and 1950s, most department stores and dime stores had a luncheonette in their design. This was before the arrival of fast food restaurants on street corners, so these stores developed the concept of having a small restaurant inside the store, usually located along one entire wall and almost always near the front entrance so shoppers walking by could see the luncheonette as they approached the store. Neighborhood drugstores copied that successful idea and also offered what were commonly referred to as lunch counters where sandwiches, hot dogs, sodas, and ice cream were sold.

In 1925, a young entrepreneur named Nick Paleveda partnered with typesetter Ollie Bryant to open his first print shop at 2101 North Florida Avenue (pictured above). Of note is the four-digit telephone number on the company car. Nick was a natural at salesmanship, making friends with every customer. In 1930, he bought out his partner and opened the Paleveda Printing Company at 909 Tampa Street. The printing business was a family affair with his wife and all of their children working there. Pictured below inside the shop in 1958 are Nick's wife, Magdalen (left), and their daughter Anna Mary.

In 1939, Nick Paleveda decided to expand his shop and moved to the company's landmark location at 102 South Tampa Street (pictured above in 1946). It was here that the print shop would become a local favorite for businessmen needing triplicate forms and politicians ordering posters. For over 75 years, three generations of the Paleveda family operated the company, making it another legendary Tampa success story. Pictured below in 1960 at the office are, from left to right, Pat Paleveda, Anna Mary Paleveda, and Joe Paleveda.

The Creighton Brothers Awning Company success story begins in 1920 when a young sailmaker from England decided to move his family to Tampa and open his own shop in the developing port city. Capt. James Coe Creighton founded the Creighton Sail Company, specializing in custom sail design. The popular sailmaker soon realized there was much more potential in the canvas awning trade. In 1941, he established the Creighton Brothers Awning Company at 103 South Franklin Street, pictured above in 1948. The company flourished during Tampa's record expansion of the 1950s, covering every type of business from diners to dress shops. Five generations of the Creighton family have worked at the awning company, which is considered Tampa's oldest.

Here is something never seen anymore—neighborhood, family-owned loan companies. This 1948 photograph captures the Hartsfield Loan Company at 128 Lafayette Street. The store is covered in neon signs advertising low-cost loans, personal loans, and immediate furniture loans. The neon sign under the canopy simply provides the last name of the owner—Hartsfield.

Pictured here in 1948 is the Darling Department Store at 507 North Franklin Street. The storefront is decorated for Christmas with strings of lights flanking the facade and Christmas wreaths hanging inside the storefront windows. On display are ladies' clothing on the left and men's clothing on the right. The small lighted booth at the main entrance of the store would usually have some featured sale items on display. (HCPLC.)

Here is the Tampa Photo Supply shop at 510 North Tampa Street in 1968. Many downtown shoppers bought their first camera here from photographer Bob Weekley, who operated the store. His wife, Rose Weekley, was also an accomplished photographer who was a favorite at churches and schools around the city.

This nighttime scene captures the
O'Neal Furniture Company at 1011
North Franklin Street in 1954. The
storefront windows reveal the latest
in home furnishings of the 1950s,
including the very popular tropical
look of the bamboo living room
furniture on display along with
several 1950s-model refrigerators and
stoves. The Tampa city directory
listed the operators of the store
as Wynstan and James O'Neal.

Here is The Outlet store at 1001
North Franklin Street, pictured
in 1948. This store specialized in
ladies' clothing and was a popular
destination in downtown for over
30 years. In the storefront windows
there are elegant displays of 1940s-
style dresses, mink coats, bathing
suits, and women's accessories.

Here is the Merry Togs shop at 917 North Franklin Street in 1959 with several ladies out window shopping for bargains. The sign uses the 19th-century term *togs*, an old English synonym for *clothing*. This store sold clothing for infants and children.

The Schwobilt store at 513 North Franklin Street is pictured in 1957. This store offered fine menswear, and in the storefront window is an elegant display of 1950s suits and ties. Notable is the elaborate Art Deco design of the storefront and neon sign. The tile work at the entrance included the store name in its design, a popular trend for downtown storefronts that allowed pedestrian traffic to notice the store name as they walked by. Simon Schwobilt established his first men's clothing store in 1912. Based in Columbus, Georgia, he later expanded, opening stores in the southeastern United States. Schwobilt's specialized in men's suits, topcoats, and overcoats. Their store motto was, "Schwobilt Suits the South." (HCPLC.)

The Lerner's ladies' dress shop in the 700 block of Franklin Street is pictured in 1941. Lerner's was a fixture for nearly 40 years in downtown Tampa. These amazing pictures capture some interesting details, including the sign in the storefront window advertising new dresses from $2.95 to $4.95. Of note are the elaborate, elegant window dressings and the two second-floor windows that were converted to storefront windows with each dramatically displaying a single dress. (HCPLC.)

It is a busy day for shoppers along Franklin Street, pictured here in 1959. This scene looks north between Twiggs and Zack Streets near Maas Brothers Department Store. Among the many shops nearby are S.H. Kress, Bakers Shoes, Haber's, and National Shirt Shops.

In this bustling scene from 1957, the Viola Todd dress shop at the corner of Tampa and Twiggs Streets is surrounded by shoppers. Viola Todd specialized in fine ladies' clothing, evening gowns, fur coats, cocktail dresses, hats, gloves, and purses. A Tampa meter maid is making her way along Twiggs Street to check the cars. Another vintage item is the monument-style concrete street marker on the corner designed for pedestrian traffic as well as motorists. The image below was taken inside the dress shop in 1942, and there are no clothing racks; rather, the store attendant would bring over the dress selected by the customer. Operated by the Kressler family, Viola Todd's was one of the city's premiere dress shops for over 30 years.

When Pio Guerra Jr. opened the Hub Liquor Store in 1946, he unknowingly founded what would become Tampa's most legendary gathering spot. The picture above was taken in 1949 shortly after the liquor store was expanded with a cocktail lounge featuring live piano music and the highest-quality drinks around. Originally located at 701 North Florida Avenue, the nightclub catered to an eclectic crowd, including bankers, judges, attorneys, mob bosses, and local airmen from MacDill Air Force Base. The scene below captures the inside of the nightclub in 1956 with a crowd of patrons seated at the bar. Notable are the vintage tabletop jukeboxes on the bar. The Hub is Tampa's oldest family-owned cocktail lounge, still operating in downtown Tampa at 719 North Franklin Street.

In 1956, Pasquale Deyorio purchased the Hub Bar and Liquor Store from the original owner and set out to offer the strongest cocktail in Tampa for the best price. The picture above looking north on Florida Avenue was taken in 1955. The Hub Bar and Liquor Store operated at the corner of Florida Avenue and Zack Street for 56 years. In the scene below from 1956, store owner Pasquale Deyorio (standing) is pictured with family and friends inside the bar. Over the years, the Hub has catered to a diverse clientele, including artists, musicians, downtown office workers, and students from the nearby college. The Hub remains family owned with many employees who have been with the store for over 25 years, including current owner Ferrell Melton, who began working there as a teenager and bought the business in 2008.

Pictured in 1939 is the Home Furniture Company at 1007 North Franklin Street, established in 1932 by Maurice Stein. The furniture company offered in-house financing to Tampa residents who were struggling during the Great Depression but needed to furnish their homes in hard times. The store flourished for over 40 years and became a downtown fixture, furnishing thousands of Tampa homeowners with high-quality furniture that they would have never been able to afford normally. The Stein family has a long history in the Tampa furniture business. Maurice's father, David Stein, opened his first store in Ybor City in 1924. All of his children were in the furniture business, including his other son Sam, who worked at the People's Furniture Store on North Florida Avenue in the 1950s, and his daughter Lena, who established the Standard Furniture Company in St. Petersburg with the assistance of David and Maurice Stein.

The Radio Bargain Shop is pictured in 1950 at 202 North Franklin Street. Inside the store is a fine selection of floor-model radios that were very popular at the time. When this photograph was taken, most homes in Tampa did not have a television. During the 1940s and 1950s, Tampa residents often gathered around the radio listening to their favorite shows for entertainment. This was the golden age of radio before televisions made their way into living rooms. Among the many favorites were *The Jack Benny Show, The Danny Kaye Show, The Milton Berle Show, The Red Skelton Show, The Amos 'n' Andy Show, The Burns and Allen Show, The Shadow, Dick Tracy,* and *The Roy Rogers Show.*

Longtime Tampa residents will remember Jensen's menswear store at 400 Franklin Street, pictured here in 1954. It is a busy day with shoppers lining the sidewalks. Jensen's sold men's suits, hats, shoes, and other clothing. The 1951 city directory listed Ira P. Krebs as president of the well-known store along with Lemuel P. Clements Jr. as vice president and Lemuel P. Clements Sr. as secretary. (HCPLC.)

Stein's Clothing Store at the northwest corner of Franklin and Twiggs Streets is pictured in 1954. Stein's offered fine menswear and women's clothing. The shoppers walking by are all well dressed with the ladies wearing dresses and gentlemen in suits and ties. Next door is the well-known Duval Jewelry Company.

The Saltz Shoe Store on the southeast corner of Tampa and Twiggs Streets is pictured in 1973. The popular shoe store was another downtown fixture for decades at this corner location. Next door is Red Cross Shoes. Both of these were among the last stores operating downtown in the early 1970s. This vintage building still stands today.

The Wolf Brothers menswear store is another legendary Tampa success story that begins with the arrival of Fred Wolf in 1889, joined by his brother Morris in 1893. The Wolf brothers had worked for many years at their uncle's dry goods store in Louisville, Kentucky. They originally worked for the Maas family before opening their own store at 808 North Franklin Street in March 1901, beginning what would become a prosperous business venture and well-known menswear store for decades. These 1958 pictures capture the storefront windows and the mezzanine level inside the store where an assortment of gentlemen's gifts are on display, including luggage, briefcases, and bar accessories. (Both, HCPLC.)

This 1952 scene captures a busy day along the crowded sidewalks of downtown Tampa between Twiggs and Zack Streets looking north along Franklin Street. Many of the ladies can be seen holding shopping bags filled with goods. This image captures the typical downtown scene of the 1950s. Among the notable businesses pictured are Haber's, National Shirt Shops, Ferrell Jewelers, and the Exchange National Bank with its distinctive Art Deco–designed building that features large octagon and round windows across the facade. Of note is how well dressed the crowd appears with ladies in their gloves and gentlemen wearing ties and hats.

Customers of this store were welcomed by Patrick and Frances Tarone. Pictured here in 1955 is the Tarone Business Machines store at 912 Grand Central Avenue (now Kennedy Boulevard). In the storefront window is an assortment of vintage cash registers and adding machines along with specially designed tables to support the machines.

The little bakery pictured here in 1946 was called the Kake Kitchen and was located at 2107 Grand Central Avenue (now Kennedy Boulevard). The storefront windows are decorated for Christmas and lined with cakes, pies, breads, and pastries. There is a vintage aluminum Christmas tree in the corner of the storefront window at right.

Here is a magnificent downtown scene from 1946. This view captures Franklin Street looking south from the intersection of Cass Street. In this photograph are many places well remembered and frequented by longtime Tampa residents. Looking to the left and continuing clockwise are the Woolworth's building, Walgreens, Butler's Shoes, Tampa Theatre, Maas Brothers Department Store, the Florida Theatre, O'Falk's Department Store, J.C. Penney Company, and the Goff Jewelry Company. There is a neon sign on the very top of the Citizen's Building—the tallest appearing here—advertising travel destinations for Tampa residents as "America's Big Three—Grand Canyon, Niagara Falls, and Silver Springs." (HCPLC.)

Pictured in 1950 is one of Tampa's most beloved variety stores—Grant's. Located at the northeast corner of Franklin and Cass Streets, Grant's was a landmark store in downtown for nearly 40 years. Everyone remembers Grant's, and one vivid memory is going down into the basement toy department to select a new doll or comic book. In the above image, the well-dressed shoppers are all wearing hats. The scene below was taken inside the store at the luncheonette in 1951 where hot fudge sundaes were only 35¢. Most downtown department stores had short-order restaurants inside them during the 1940s and 1950s. Many longtime Tampa residents will remember the hot dogs offered at this restaurant, considered the best in downtown. (Both, USFSCL.)

The J.J. Newberry Company, another favorite Tampa dime store, is pictured in 1950. This store was located at the southeast corner of Franklin and Cass Streets in one of Tampa's landmark Art Deco–style structures of the 1940s. Above the main entrance is the sign that reads, "5-10-25¢." This was a popular method of signage for dime stores during this era because most of the goods sold there were close to these pricing points. The 1950 photograph below was taken inside the J.J. Newberry store near the candy department. It is a busy day with shoppers browsing through the aisles and several ladies heading into the basement level. (Both, USFSCL.)

43

This photograph will certainly surprise today's teenagers with a rare glimpse of popular fashions from the 1940s designed for Tampa's high school crowd. This is the Teenage Hall clothing store at 207 Twiggs Street, pictured in 1947. The store has decorated their window with the latest styles worn at school dances, including gowns for the girls and suits for the boys. (USFSCL.)

This busy scene from 1952 captures several popular stores on the east side of Franklin Street looking south near Cass Street. Shoppers can be seen strolling along the sidewalk in front of J.J. Newberry's, Boyd's Shoe, and S.H. Kress. Farther down the street are Woolworth's and the Tampa Theatre building with its original neon sign lighting up the boulevard.

Pictured here in 1949 is the Morton-Williams Department Store at the northwest corner of Florida Avenue and Twiggs Street. The bustling scene captures shoppers enjoying their day downtown. Notable are the vintage Christmas decorations inside the storefront windows and the newspaper stand on the corner. This store sold clothing, shoes, and hats.

This classic scene from December 1952 captures the glimmering lights of downtown Tampa looking north along Franklin Street from Zack Street. Notable are the elaborate Christmas decorations Tampa had strung across the streets. Among the many stores seen are O'Falk's Department Store and Butler's Shoes. Two of downtown's most popular theaters can be seen here with the Florida Theatre entrance on the left and the Tampa Theatre entrance on the right. Longtime Tampa residents will remember spending their allowance at these theaters on Saturdays for matinees in air-conditioning, which was a special treat because most homes did not have cooling systems during the 1950s. The Florida Theatre owner made a special arrangement with the Tampa Theatre owner to share his air-conditioning by installing a series of underground pipes below Franklin Street that would cool his theater on hot summer days.

In 1945, A.S. Leroy opened his Sinclair Service Station (pictured above) in 1947 at 207 Morgan Street. The young entrepreneur was a smart businessman who wanted an edge over other gas stations, so he started a new concept in automobile service: a mobile lubrication truck that he could drive to any business with a fleet of delivery vans or trucks. He was a favorite service center for the local AAA office, which sent him all the downtown calls. Always going the extra mile, Leroy made friends with every customer. During the 1946 hurricane that struck Tampa, Leroy kept his station open 24 hours for evacuees and also offered up his service trucks for the American Red Cross to use in recovery efforts. In the 1948 image below, A.S. Leroy poses in the back of his service truck after winning the Sinclair Dealer of the Month award.

On Friday nights, A.S. Leroy turned his gas station parking lot into a movie theater for neighborhood children, as seen in this 1947 photograph. His two young sons Gene and Glenn were always at their dad's side at the station and would help serve ice cream and cake to the many children arriving for the show.

Leroy's Sinclair Service Station was a family affair with A.S.'s wife, Pansy Leroy, running the office and their baby's crib right behind the counter. In this 1947 picture, Pansy is busy handling the books with her handy electric adding machine nearby on the desk. A.S. Leroy operated his friendly service station for over 15 years in downtown Tampa and remained in the service station business for over 50 years.

Mrs. Pansy LeRoy plays an important part in her husband's success by taking care of books, follow-up systems, etc.

This scene from 1952 captures the busy intersection of Madison and Franklin Streets looking north. It is a busy day for shoppers, and there are many stores and shops lining both sides of Franklin Street, including, from the left side of the photograph, Madison Drugs at its original location, Magnon Jewelers, Weil-Maas Department Store, Duval Jewelry Company, Mangel's, and Maas Brothers Department Store. Looking to the right are the Mills Loan Company and the Darling Department Store. Most of the stores and shops situated between the large department stores along Franklin Street were small, family-owned businesses that thrived for many years.

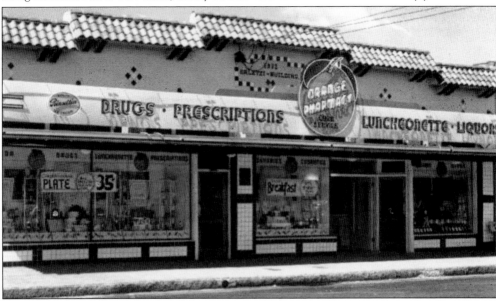

Pictured in 1942 is the Orange Pharmacy at 2113 Grand Central Avenue with its elaborate display of neon signs stretching across the entire storefront. In the storefront window is an advertisement for a complete lunch at the store luncheonette for 35¢. Luncheonettes were a type of short-order restaurant where shoppers could stop to enjoy a quick cup of coffee and piece of pie when it was time to take a break from shopping. Most neighborhood drugstores had luncheonettes inside them during the 1940s and 1950s before the arrival of fast food restaurants on street corners.

Shea and Prange Drugs was one of Tampa's legendary drugstores, pictured here in 1952 at its 702 Grand Central Avenue location. The storefront tells a story of much simpler times with a luncheonette and the 5-10-25¢ store advertisements above the windows. The store's restaurant was a popular lunchtime gathering spot for University of Tampa students who were just a few blocks away. The store was family owned for decades. The 1951 city directory lists Thomas J. and Carl Shea as owners, Edmund L. Shea and Herbert Shea as managers, and Richard Shea as clerk.

This busy scene is looking north along Florida Avenue at Royal Street in 1957. The rooftop billboard is a classic 1950s advertisement for Pepsi-Cola still using their original vintage bottle-cap logo. The giant bottle cap was over 20 feet tall and made entirely of neon in a Broadway-style light show that could be seen for miles. Among the businesses in this building are a hardware store, bookshop, and furniture store. The vintage building pictured here still stands today, one of the few remaining from Tampa's early years.

These 1946 images capture the Plant Park Pharmacy along Lafayette Street (now Kennedy Boulevard) looking east toward downtown Tampa. In the above scene are several businesses, including the Park Theatre and Gatteri Photo Supply. The scene below captures a gentleman checking the headlines, and in the storefront window is an advertisement for grilled steak sandwiches for only 20¢ at the store's luncheonette. The store also has complete breakfasts, lunches, or dinners advertised for 25¢–35¢ per plate. This vintage building still stands today.

Two

SEMINOLE HEIGHTS AND NORTH TAMPA

Pictured in 1968 is the legendary Sulphur Springs Hotel arcade. This rare photograph was taken from the north end of the covered, first-floor promenade looking south and provides a close-up view of the terrazzo walkway and detailed archways that created such an architectural gem. Originally completed in 1927, this building remained the center of all activity in Sulphur Springs for 50 years and was considered the first indoor shopping venue in the state. Situated on the southwest corner of North Nebraska Avenue and Bird Street, the massive structure occupied an entire city block. At one time, the building received some distinguished notoriety when *Ripley's Believe It Or Not* designated the structure as the "nation's only complete city under one roof."

Longtime Tampa residents will remember the popular Simon's Studio at 4602 North Florida Avenue, pictured here in 1952. This photography studio was one of Tampa's busiest, taking tens of thousands of photographs for schools and churches all around the city. The studio also offered in-home portraits and photographed thousands of Tampa couples on their wedding day.

This little grocery store was very busy with shoppers when this photograph was taken in 1940. Corner stores were popular during this era because there were very few large supermarkets around the city at this time. The Self Service Store was at 6501 North Central Avenue in the heart of Seminole Heights. It was owned by the Spear family and offered groceries, a meat market, and fresh produce. Their delivery van is parked out front, ready to deliver telephone orders to the many families that did not have cars in the neighborhood. At far left, you can just see the gable from the front of the house. The vintage building and that house are both still standing.

The Publix Supermarket at 6001 Nebraska Avenue can be seen in 1950, shortly after its construction. This Art Deco structure featured twin covered walkways that projected down the center of both side parking lots to assist shoppers on rainy days. In 1995, the store was demolished and replaced with a larger building that was carefully designed to replicate the vintage architectural details of the original structure. This area of Seminole Heights became a flourishing business district during the 1950s with many motels and shops lining both sides of Nebraska Avenue. The area saw much development during that era because Nebraska Avenue was one of only two main thoroughfares leading into the city from the north.

This 1948 image captures the Hillsborough Pharmacy located at the corner of East Hillsborough and Nebraska Avenues, a Seminole Heights fixture for over 30 years. The storefront windows have shampoo advertised for 35¢, and jars of aspirin are on sale for 59¢. The sidewalk sign is promoting milk shakes at the store's soda fountain.

Pictured in 1940 is Alpine Liquor Store, Seminole Heights's oldest, most favorite liquor store. In 1936, Al Manolt Sr. moved his family from Alpine, New Jersey, and decided to open a new liquor store in Tampa, naming it after his hometown. He bought an old wooden building at 7501 Nebraska Avenue for $3,200 and opened a bar where he also sold package liquors, served hamburgers, and offered slot machines to customers while they waited. In the photograph above, cook Mac Williams (left) and bartender Jimmy Crowell are taking drink orders from customers who were served curbside. Cleverly attached to the tall pine tree is the giant neon sign that reads, "AL." In the scene below from 1937, Al Manolt Sr. (far right) is celebrating the first anniversary of his store's opening with customers and staff.

To celebrate the 25th anniversary of the business in 1961, the Manolt family announced plans for a modern, larger store to be built on the existing property. In 1962, Alpine Liquors proudly opened their new two-story liquor store accented with a flashy new neon sign that incorporated the vintage, 1936 Art Deco clock from the old storefront, as seen below. Four generations of the Manolt family have operated this successful venture and continue to welcome loyal customers, many of whom still recall driving up for curbside service in the 1950s. The picture above from 1964 captures the storefront with an overflowing parking lot of 1960s classics parked out front.

Clark's Drugstore, located at the northwest corner of North Florida and Buffalo Avenues (now Martin Luther King Drive), appears in this 1948 image. The store also had a cafeteria and soda fountain, very common in corner drugstores around the country during this era. This must have been a popular hangout for students from the nearby Hillsborough High School for after-school snacks, burgers, and sodas. The city directory lists Ernest V. Clark as owner and Earl Miller as the store pharmacist. The building still stands today and is home to Seminole Heights High School.

Here is the Florida Avenue Market in the 4800 block of Florida Avenue in 1950. Established by Charles Schiro in 1944, the market was one of the neighborhood's most popular, offering a butcher shop, fresh fruit, ice cream, and other groceries. The family all shared in running the store, including Charles's wife, Naomi, and sons Charles Jr., Ronnie, and Gary. The store operated for nearly 30 years before closing in 1972. Some nostalgic items in the picture are the bushels of fruit and the sign for Florida Dairy and Holsum Bakery—two iconic Tampa companies with legendary success stories.

Longtime Seminole Heights residents will fondly remember Lang's Ice Cream Parlor and Soda Shop at the corner of North Florida and Osborne Avenues, pictured below in 1951. The shop was established in 1945 by L.F. Lang and his son Stu Lang, who designed a unique ice cream maker that produced little, square ice cream pops. This was a popular hangout for students from nearby Hillsborough High School. Friends gathered after school for ice cream sundaes and milk shakes. The Lang's Hyde Park location at 402 South Howard Avenue is pictured above in 1952. The scene below captures the Seminole Heights store's vintage ice cream bus, which was popular at birthday parties. Children could come inside the bus and select their favorite treats.

Here is the Leggett Music Company, located at 3114 Florida Avenue in 1956. Leggett's was one of Tampa's best-known music stores during the 1950s, supplying pianos and organs to dozens of churches, schools, and funeral homes. During the 1940s, Harold Leggett was helping his father expand their music company in West Palm Beach, eventually opening 13 stores along the east coast of Florida. In 1947, Harold married his sweetheart Virginia, and the couple decided to open their own music store in Tampa. In 1948, the Leggett Music Company was established and would flourish during Tampa's major expansion and growth of the 1950s. Harold Leggett carefully chose a location situated between the city's two largest high schools—Jefferson High in Tampa Heights and Hillsborough High in Seminole Heights. His music store was filled with band instruments and supplied flutes, guitars, violins, drums, clarinets, and trumpets to hundreds of students. In the photograph below from 1958, Virginia Leggett (left) is showing a new piano to a potential customer.

Pictured in 1956 is the grand opening of the organ salon inside the Leggett Music Company, featuring an organ concert at the salon's music studio. Seated next to each other in the second row are Harold and Virginia Leggett (second and third from left), who owned the company from 1948 to 1962. In the scene below from 1957, the company delivery truck is being loaded with some new upright pianos for the store. Leggett's was one of Tampa's most popular music stores during the 1950s—a time when everyone was sending their children to piano lessons and many families enjoyed gathering around the organ in their living rooms to hear a nostalgic tune.

The Allied Linoleum and Floor Covering Company at 5134 North Florida Avenue in Seminole Heights is pictured in 1950. The store is advertising some popular mid-century products, including venetian blinds and asphalt tile, both commonly used in new home construction around Tampa during the 1950s.

The owners of this produce stand were so proud of their venture they named it Our New Market. Pictured here in 1945, the little open-air market was located at 7204 Nebraska Avenue in Seminole Heights. Tomatoes are priced at four for 25¢.

The Oldt Waring Appliance store at 4510 North Florida Avenue is pictured in 1957, and there is a fine selection of new, 1950s-model Frigidaire appliances on display in the storefront windows. Other businesses seen along the block include the Lee Duncan Insurance Agency and a tropical fish store. This area in Seminole Heights was a popular shopping district during the 1950s. The building pictured here still stands today.

The C.J. Stoll Trailer Company at 7200 North Nebraska Avenue in Seminole Heights is pictured in 1958. This photograph offers a rare view of vintage travel trailers and mid-century mobile homes. The showroom is designed with floor-to-ceiling windows much like an automobile showroom to allow passing motorists a view of the trailers. The business was advertised as "the world's largest indoor trailer store." This location was perfect for such a business because Nebraska Avenue was the main thoroughfare used by travelers from the north arriving in Tampa during the 1950s before the interstate system was constructed.

In 1949, Casimir Lesiak moved his family from Scranton, Pennsylvania, to build Pickford's Sundries at 2606 West Hillsborough Avenue. He chose the name Pickford's because he felt the family name was too difficult for customers to pronounce and was a big fan of silent film star Mary Pickford. The drugstore became one of Tampa's most well known for over 50 years and was one of the last family-owned drugstores of that era, encompassing the lives of many people who grew up in West Tampa and Seminole Heights during the 1950s. Many Tampa children spent their allowances buying comics, toys, sodas, ice cream sundaes, and MoonPies at this neighborhood drugstore. The above scene captures the storefront in 1955. Pictured below at the storefront window in 1968 are Casimir's son Cas Lesiak and his wife, Jo, who operated the store. Casimir's other children Frank and Mary also worked there at times.

During the 1950s, neighborhood friends met at Pickford's on a daily basis and became one extended family. Pictured here in 1958 are the "Pickford Kids," a group of neighborhood children who all lived on the street behind the store and met after school at the store's lunch counter for ice cream sodas and milk shakes. From left to right are (first row) Sadie Jackson, Sharon Wolcott, Mike Gaskins, Gregory Jackson, Johnny Lilly, Gary Jackson, and Mike Alfonso; (second row) Mary Jackson, Earl Finch, James Finch, Bobby Floyd, Cas Lesiak, and Ralph Gaskins. In April 2009, the vintage building was completely restored, opened as the Custom Creations Café-Bakery, and is still operating there today. The image below from 1968 captures the luncheonette inside the store with advertisements for ice cream sundaes, banana splits, soups, and sandwiches.

Penney's
ALWAYS FIRST QUALITY
EOM
end-of-month clean-up

NORTH GATE ONLY!

FIRST COME! FIRST SERVED!
Some items are very limited . . . broken sizes unless otherwise noted!
Sorry! No phone or mail orders, please!

Hurry! Only 150 reduced to clear . . .
WOMEN'S BETTER DRESSES
Giant mark-downs to make room for Spring stocks! Save! . . . . . . **2**⁷⁷ to **8**⁷⁷

60 only! Packaged budget dresses. 2.8⁸
250 only! Women's pinwale corduroy jumpers . . . 2.4⁴
100 only! Women's better sleepwear. 1.8⁸

Hurry! Only 185 at this price . . .
WOMEN'S COTTON DUSTERS
Ideal gift item. Choose from shifts, embossed, more **1**²²

In April 1955, Tampa mayor Curtis Hixon broke ground on what was considered the largest shopping center in the state. Northgate Shopping Center was situated on a 30-acre parcel at 8800 North Florida Avenue in North Tampa. Northgate opened in the fall of 1956 and was a welcome sight for residents in Seminole Heights, who had to plan all their shopping trips for downtown Tampa where they would have to pay for parking and struggle with their packages on rainy days. With the opening of Northgate, all those troubles were forgotten. This new shopping plaza offered all the popular stores and shops of the day along with free parking and covered walkways. Developers appropriately named the shopping center Northgate because it was situated in a developing area of the city where major population growth and construction were under way.

This advertisement for the J.C. Penney store location at Northgate Shopping Center appeared in the *Tampa Tribune* on November 21, 1962. The other large stores in the plaza included W.T. Grant's, Poller's Dress Shop, Eggner-Diaz menswear store, Neisner's Variety Store, and Publix Supermarket. Among the advertised prices here are new ladies' dresses for $2.77 each, corduroy jumpers for $2.44 each, and women's sleepwear on sale for $1.88.

This 1956 scene captures shoppers in front of Madison's Drugs, one of Tampa's most memorable drugstores with a longtime presence in downtown Tampa. This location was at the new Northgate Shopping Center and was among several locations that opened in shopping plazas around the city during the 1950s.

Many of today's younger generation will have no idea how this store operated. Pictured in 1956 is the S&H Green Stamps Store at Northgate. Smart businesses around the city knew that customers would often frequent their establishment, and the little green stamps were offered at supermarkets, gas stations, and drugstores. Every spare coffee pot and cookie jar in the house could not avoid these little gems, and they brought such excitement to shoppers who would dutifully take their filled S&H Green Stamp booklets to this store with plans for a new toaster or set of dishes.

Pictured in 1956, Lazzara's Courtesy Market at 4901 Nebraska Avenue was a Seminole Heights landmark for 45 years. In 1936, Ralph Lazzara Jr. bought the lot for $150 and built his new market, selling fresh produce, meats, Cuban bread, sandwiches, sodas, beer, candy, fresh flowers, and many exotic fruits that could not be had elsewhere. This was Tampa's first open-air supermarket open 24 hours a day. The Lazzara success story begins in the early 20th century on the Lazzara farm in Ybor City where Ralph Lazzara Sr. and his wife, Mary, had nine children who all worked on the farm, but their seven boys had a special duty of each pushing a produce cart around neighborhoods selling fresh fruits and vegetables. In the picture below from 1957, Ralph Lazzara Jr. and his wife, Mary, are pictured in front of their market, which had potatoes on sale—10 for 50¢.

Here is Ralph Lazzara Jr. at the age of 20, proudly showing off his new delivery truck for Lazzara's Courtesy Market in 1940. His four children all worked at the store along with his wife, Mary. In the scene below from 1960, the couple is inside the market at 4901 Nebraska Avenue. Lazzara's Courtesy Market had the largest selection of fresh produce in the area with well-stocked aisles of canned goods and sundries that other markets did not offer. The store sold bananas for 5¢ a pound, attracting housewives from all over the city with plans for puddings, breads, and pies. In 1962, the store made local headlines when the television program *Candid Camera* taped a stunt inside the store with Allen Funt trying to purchase some bananas that he claimed were already peeled when he arrived at the store.

When this new Sears store opened in 1958 at the northwest corner of East Hillsborough Avenue and Twenty-second Street, it was a welcome sight for residents of Seminole Heights and North Tampa. At that time, there were no department stores in the area, so the store opened with much fanfare and celebration. Residents flocked to the massive multilevel store that offered the convenience of free parking with covered walkways and an array of expanded favorite departments. The toy department is a vivid memory for longtime Tampa folks who will recall the giant treasure chests filled to the brim and the toy train villages that were set up at Christmastime. The most distinguishing feature of the iconic building was the aeronautic design of the roofline, which was very popular in commercial architecture of the 1950s. The building still stands today and is home to the Erwin Vocational School.

Nostalgic Tampa residents will fondly remember Holsum Bakery at the corner of East Hillsborough Avenue and Twenty-second Street, pictured here in 1949. Christmas was a citywide celebrated event with an open house featuring tours of the decorated bakery, sweet treats, free candy, and little miniature loaves of fresh-baked Holsum bread for everyone along with fresh fruits and cookies.

The S.S. Kresge Company was a well-established dime-store chain predominantly in the Midwest and Northeast. By 1960, the Kresge Stores were lagging behind Woolworth's and Kress in sales, and the company decided to expand into what would become the discount-store business, introducing K-Mart, a large discount department store that featured departments not commonly found in other department stores, such as sporting goods, appliances, home improvement, television-radio, and automotive supplies. Many locations also had supermarkets inside them, and all stores featured a luncheonette. In 1962, the Kresge Company opened the first K-Mart discount store and continued to open an average of 35 stores per year through the end of the 1960s. Pictured here is the K-Mart located in the Sulphur Springs neighborhood of Tampa in 1964 at the corner of Florida Avenue and Bird Street, still operating today.

Frank Cinchett was a pioneer in the neon sign industry, opening his first shop in 1927 in Philadelphia. By 1947, the sign industry was crowded in that city, so Frank decided to move his sign company to Tampa, setting up shop at 4707 North Florida Avenue, pictured above in 1951. Frank and his son John F. Cinchett became masters of their trade, building thousands of neon signs for every type of business around the city. Many of their neon signs featured elaborate animated designs that became local landmarks. Frank was a skilled artist who brought his colorful ideas to life through neon and introduced a Broadway style of neon craftsmanship that Tampa had not seen before. In the 1957 image below, John F. Cinchett (far left) is building a neon sign inside the shop. Frank Cinchett is third from left, wearing his signature bow tie.

Pictured above in 1959 is John F. Cinchett building neon marquees for the well-known Chez Louie nightclub. A large pattern is laid out on the workbench. The creator of a neon sign is an artist because it is the design of the sign taken from a drawn pattern that the neon glass is formed upon. During the 1950s, the sign company also offered in-house financing on neon signs—something never done before in Tampa—which allowed small business owners to afford the large neon signs they normally would have had to forego. That charitable philosophy created a legendary success story for the company, which operated for 50 years in Seminole Heights. In 1982, the sign shop became a third-generation family-operated business when Frank's grandchildren Diana and Johnny Cinchett and James Blount all worked there. Pictured below in 1956 is Frank Cinchett designing another flashy neon sign inside his office.

The Olin Mott Tire Company's success story begins in 1954 when a young, entrepreneurial tire company executive from Macon, Georgia, decided to realize his dream and open his own tire shop in Tampa. After 18 months of researching potential cities, Olin Mott selected Tampa, which was experiencing record population growth and offered great potential for the fortuitous business venture he planned in the retread market. In an alliance with the nationally known Tampa Golden Gate Speedway racetrack, the tire company heavily promoted the quality of the retread tire with a guarantee of new tire mileage and appearance. In 1955, Olin Mott opened his first tire shop at the Elkes Pontiac dealership on Florida Avenue in downtown Tampa. A year later, on January 2, 1956, his dream became reality with the grand opening of his first self-standing tire store, the Elkes-Mott Tire Company at 3741 East Hillsborough Avenue, pictured above. In 1960, the company dissolved the partnership with Elkes Pontiac and officially became the Olin Mott Tire Company, pictured below in 1965.

Since 1955, the Olin Mott Tire Company has been well known in the city of Tampa for its dedication to the support and sponsorship of community outreach programs. Employees are considered extended family and greet everyone with the company slogan, "It's a great day at Olin Mott!" Four generations of the Mott family will share in the proven approach that has brought the company renowned local success, growing to six Tampa-area locations and expanding the original location from 5,000 square feet to a massive 50,000-square-foot business complex that serves as company headquarters. Pictured above is the North Florida Avenue location in 1962, which still operates today. In the photograph below, also taken in 1962, company employees are, from left to right, Dutch Wingert, Bill Ballard, Olin Mott, Harry Hudson, Carmen Cacamo, Terry Moore, and Henry Clayburn.

Here is the Armenia Shopping Center at the northwest corner of Armenia and Sligh Avenues in 1958 shortly after its grand opening. North Tampa celebrated the opening of many shopping centers during the 1950s as the neighborhoods continued to see record-setting population growth. In this plaza were several popular stores of this era, including Spotless Cleaners, Madison Drugs, the Belk-Lindsey Department Store, and the B&B Supermarket. The busy plaza still stands today. (HCPLC.)

Here is the new J.M. Fields Department Store shortly after its opening in 1958. Located at the northeast corner of Florida Avenue and Temple Terrace Highway (now Busch Boulevard), this store was another addition to the fast developing Florida Avenue shopping district in North Tampa. J.M. Fields featured a mix of merchandise found in most of today's modern-day discount retailers—housewares, clothing, sporting goods, electronics, and lawn and garden. The popular department store chain was expanding along the East Coast and opened many stores in Florida between 1958 and 1961. The J.M. Fields chain of stores all closed in 1978. (HCPLC.)

The Zayre Department Store chain expanded heavily during the early 1960s. By 1966, Zayre had 92 stores nationwide with three stores in Tampa, including the location at 2525 East Hillsborough Avenue, pictured here in 1962. One of the distinctive features of the store design was the massive sign that would flank the entire length of the storefront in very tall neon letters with just the name *Zayre*. The company's original tagline commonly used in their advertising was "Zayre—Fabulous Department Store." The stores carried typical wares, such as toys, records, domestics, linens, cosmetics, household items, and an expanded clothing line for men and women. The final closing of all Zayre stores occurred in October 1989 when the Ames store chain acquired the remaining locations.

The Pee Gee Paint Store at 2800 North Florida Avenue is pictured in 1948. The store is all lit up at night with an elaborate neon sign display that stretches across the entire storefront. This area of Florida Avenue was a popular business district during the 1940s and 1950s because it was one of the main thoroughfares leading out of downtown Tampa into the north end of the city.

Here is Springs Photo Service at the corner of Grant Avenue and North Nebraska Avenue in Sulphur Springs in 1956. The large neon sign (shaped into a giant numeral 5) above the building advertises five-hour photograph service. Parked out front are the store's delivery vehicles. The shop was opened in 1952 by local photographer Sam Sellers, who later expanded to five locations around the city. Sam was only 19 years old when he opened his first photograph shop. His son Sam Sellers Jr. joined him in the business and still operates a photograph shop today, continuing the family legacy at Golden Triangle Photography in South Tampa.

Here is the Margaret-Ann Supermarket at 8331 Nebraska Avenue near Waters Avenue in 1948. This must have been a popular store for Sulphur Springs residents because there were no other large supermarkets along Nebraska Avenue at this time. This was one of Tampa's earliest supermarket chains with five locations around the city during the 1940s.

Three

TAMPA HEIGHTS AND WEST TAMPA

The iconic Buena Vista Hotel building at the southeast corner of LaSalle Street and Garcia Avenue is pictured above in 1949. On the first floor were several stores and shops, including the Bretton Department Store and Lucida Grocery Store. The hotel was located in the Roberts City area of West Tampa and was the center of all activity for shopping and entertainment. Longtime residents will recall this hotel as a focal point in the area with a public swimming pool and large patio for dances. Roberts City was considered the first fully integrated neighborhood with black families living and socializing next to Cubans, Italians, and Spaniards. In Roberts City, a friendly weaving of cultures existed, creating lifelong friendships where no distinction of color separated the good deeds shared among neighbors. Proud memories live on in the hearts of many who recall the unique solidarity that was shared there. (HCPLC.)

Pictured in 1946 are West Tampa's two most beloved stores. The West Tampa Department Store was established by Emiliano Salcines in 1941 and became a legendary gathering spot for residents who flocked to the store not just for their clothing, but also for wise guidance and caring advice from Emiliano, who became the unofficial mayor of West Tampa. With his wife, Juanita, at his side as the store seamstress, the couple made lifelong friendships with customers for nearly 25 years. Next door at 1703 North Howard Avenue was Eagle Drugs, established by Peter Cimino Sr. in 1929. Their familiar sign can be seen on the north end of the redbrick building. The Cimino family operated Eagle Drugs for over 70 years; it became an institution for the neighborhood and is fondly remembered today by generations of Tampa families who shopped there. The scene below captures the store interior in 1940. (Above, *La Gaceta*.)

This 1957 photograph captures the corner of West Cass Street and North Rome Avenue. During the 1950s, this area was one of the busiest in West Tampa with all types of family-owned stores and shops. On the northeast corner is the Boromei-Mirabella Fish Market with several customers standing out front. The market was owned by Charlie and Jenny Mirabella and remained family operated for over 30 years. Jenny's brother Johnny Boromei established the fish company with Charlie Mirabella in 1947. The fish market was also a grocery store for the neighborhood. In later years, Charlie's sons Ernie, Frank, and Mike all worked at the store. Across the street is the Sparrow Lumber Company owned by Victor Sparrow.

Pictured here in 1950 is the Howard Avenue Hardware Company at the corner of North Howard Avenue and Green Street. The store was operated by Felino Cabrera (right) with employee Joe Puleo (left). The store opened in 1949 and flourished during Tampa's construction boom of the 1950s. For 30 years, three generations of the Cabrera family operated the store.

Pictured here in 1960 is Sam Cacciatore at his market located at 1502 Tampa Street. Sam and Mary Cacciatore opened their first store in 1934, and it quickly became a neighborhood favorite, selling groceries, produce, and fresh meats. Sam's Food Store was among many small, family-owned markets found on almost every street corner during the 1940s and 1950s before the arrival of large supermarkets. Pictured below in 1948 are, from left to right, Sam and Mary Cacciatore and her sister Fifi Nuccio standing next to the Gator Foods float in the Gasparilla Parade. Sam's Food Store was a member of the Gator Foods cooperative.

This 1950 image captures Sam Cacciatore behind
the counter inside his store at 1502 Tampa Street.
There is a fine vintage display of groceries,
cookies, and candy to enjoy. In 1954, his daughter
Joanne married local butcher Felix Lopez, and
the couple took over managing the store soon
after. In 1962, after almost 30 years in business,
the construction of Interstate 275 was announced,
and the store was directly in its path. The family
decided to move and rebuild an exact replica of
the original store at 2102 North Armenia Avenue.
Loyal customers did not mind the short drive
across the river to the new location, and the
store continued its legacy for another 25 years.

Pictured inside the market in 1956 are Joanne and
Felix Lopez who operated Sam's Food Store from
1954 to 1987. Felix Lopez also came from a Tampa
grocery family with longtime roots in Ybor City.
The couple operated the store along with Joanne's
parents, Sam and Mary Cacciatore, offering fresh
fruits, vegetables, groceries, and fresh meats with
no set closing hours at the store; they just locked
up after dinner by checking to see if anyone was
coming down the sidewalk. The store became a
third-generation, family-operated business when
the couple's daughters Gina, Julie, and Jeannette
all worked at the market with their parents.

This little building at 3400 North Florida Avenue has certainly had many lives. Pictured above in 1940, the store was home to the Southern Dairies Ice Cream Bar. Ice cream sodas are advertised in the window for 10¢. In the photograph below, taken 10 years later in 1950, the new tenant is Johnnie's Tire and Battery Shop owned by Johnnie Morris, who proudly included his name in the neon sign above the sidewalk. Vintage whitewall tires from the 1950s are on display. In later years, this building became a Mary Carter Paint Shop.

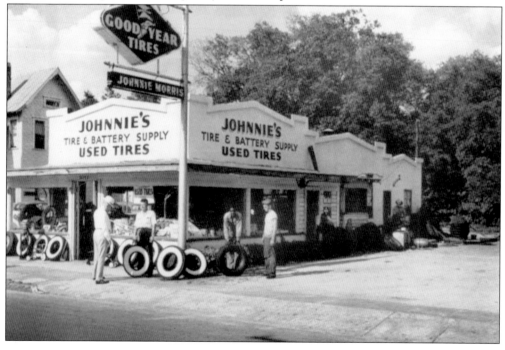

The Leone Brothers Market was a West Tampa fixture for 50 years. In 1922, Vincent and Anthony Leone opened their market at 1214 North Howard Avenue, pictured above in 1938. Standing out front are, from left to right, little Sam Leone, Anthony Leone, Vincent Leone, and employee Juan Antonio "Lulo" Lopez. The store prospered during the 1940s and 1950s before the arrival of large supermarkets. Pictured in the store in 1940 are, from left to right, Lulo Lopez, Vincent Leone, Tony Alessi, and Anthony Leone. The brothers offered groceries on credit to many regular customers, something unheard of today. Anthony's sons Sam and James Leone also worked at the store delivering groceries every day after school to many customers who called in telephone orders because they did not have a car, which was very common during this era. Three generations of the Leone family worked at the store, which closed in 1972.

The Govin family's success story began on the front porch of their Tampa Heights home in 1933. At the age of 15, Armand Govin's first job was working for the Franklin Stationery Company in 1927 where he was trained in making rubber stamps. He decided to further his training at one of New York City's largest rubber stamp manufacturers where he perfected his skills. He returned to Tampa in 1933, and with his new wife, Virginia, at his side, the young couple made Armand's dream a reality and established Govin's Rubber Stamp Company in their home at 1905 Florida Avenue. The couple filled their living room with manufacturing equipment and turned the front porch into their showroom. In 1950, they enclosed the porch and added on a storefront to the house, pictured below in 1956 with Virginia Govin behind the counter. The picture above was taken in 1969 after the storefront was expanded.

The Govin family has been supplying Tampa business offices for nearly 80 years. Pictured here in 1938 is Armand Govin making deliveries in his 1928 Ford Coupe. His wife, Virginia, took telephone orders from a makeshift storefront on the front porch of their home. The store became Tampa's most notable during the 1950s, offering rubber stamps, name tags, desk plates, stationery, forms, office furniture, and notary seals. In the 1960s, Armand's son Ron Govin took the lead in expanding the store and developed a new larger line of products. Four generations of the Govin family have operated the company since then, and it still operates today as MarkMaster, Inc., in a new, state-of-the-art, 33,000-square-foot facility in North Tampa. Pictured below is the 1976 company photograph at 1905 Florida Avenue.

Here is the Frazier's Furniture Company at 1010 North Westshore Boulevard in 1958, owned and operated by John and Marjorie Frazier. The storefront windows are filled with a fine selection of mid-century furniture and lamps. Their slogan was "Frazier's—For the Unusual at Reasonable Prices."

Pictured in 1948 is the Tanner Paint Company at 107 Tyler Street, Tampa's only drive-through paint store. The customers actually drove their cars into the store, were helped with their order, and then backed out. H.D. Tanner started his first paint store in 1933 with 2,000 gallons of paint repossessed from a bankrupt hardware store. What started out as a small business venture has led to nearly 80 years of flourishing success. In 1964, the company outgrew their little shop and expanded to build a manufacturing plant and showroom at 4917 Armenia Avenue. Four generations of the Tanner family have operated the paint company since then, and it remains the oldest family-owned paint store in the state of Florida.

Giuseppe Clementi came from a proud Sicilian family of carpenters. In 1928, he decided to open a grocery store in West Tampa at 2213 North Armenia Avenue and constructed the entire two-story building himself with living quarters upstairs, a grocery store downstairs, and an apartment behind the structure that he could rent out for extra income. Giuseppe and his wife, Rosaria, ran the store, which offered groceries, meats, sandwiches, and fresh Cuban bread for neighborhood families. In later years, their daughter Jennie Menendez would take over the store, which operated for nearly 40 years. The photograph at right was taken in 1940. Inside the store in 1941 are, from left to right, Rosaria Clementi, Jennie Menendez, and James Clementi.

Pictured in 1957 is the Super Test gas station located at 2500 North Tampa Street in Tampa Heights. Among the interesting nostalgic symbols are those vintage gas pumps. The prices advertised include gas for 29¢ a gallon, and quarts of oil are on display for 15¢ each.

This little neighborhood market was at 122 Palm Avenue in 1956, and eggs are advertised in the window on sale at three dozen for $1. That year, milk was sold here for 79¢ a gallon and bread was 18¢ a loaf. On the corner near the store entrance is a vintage fire alarm call box that Tampa had installed on street corners for emergencies.

This building looks like it just came in for a landing at 3015 Grand Central Avenue. Pictured in 1952, the Cracker Village was home to a liquor store, restaurant, lounge, and drive-in that offered curb service. Notable are the elaborate neon signs and stars surrounding the circular canopy where cars pulled under to have their orders taken—a popular design style of 1950s drive-ins.

This 1968 scene captures the West Hillsborough Plaza at the corner of Memorial Highway and Hillsborough Avenue. Among the businesses are Eckerd Drugs and the Publix Supermarket with its signature wings on the storefront. During the 1960s, Publix created an alliance with Eckerd Drugs to serve as anchor tenants in dozens of shopping centers around the state of Florida.

In September 1961, F.W. Woolworth's announced plans to expand into the discount store market with an aggressive plan to open a new chain of large stores. The department store industry was changing with the expansion of K-Mart and Zayre stores across the country. Woolworth's answer to this proposed expansion became Woolco with the first store opening in June 1962. These large, expanded department stores would offer many departments not found at Woolworth's, including expanded lines of jewelry, appliances, and clothing. The larger stores allowed for Woolworth's to offer higher-ticket items as well, such as stereo and television consoles. Pictured in 1968 is the Woolco on West Hillsborough Avenue in the Horizon Park Shopping Center. In 1982, Woolworth's sadly announced the closing of all Woolco stores following the Christmas shopping season.

Here is the Rio Italia Village in 1957 at the corner of Dale Mabry Highway and Spruce Street. The building is covered in flashy 1950s-style neon signs advertising the drive-through liquor store, cocktail lounge, and pizzeria. This liquor store was operated by the Donofrio family.

In 1960, Montgomery Ward made their presence known in Tampa with this large, multilevel department store located at 1701 North Dale Mabry Highway. The residents of West Tampa were excited about the grand opening because at that time, there were no other large department stores or shopping centers in this area of the city. Today, this parcel is occupied by a Walmart.

Here is the grand opening of the new Gulf Supermarket at 1705 North Dale Mabry Highway on July 16, 1957. The design of the building featured an elaborate 1950s-style covered promenade that stretched across the entire storefront. There is an advertisement in the storefront window for new men's sport shirts on sale for 99¢. Today, this site is home to a Best Buy electronics store.

Here is the announcement for the grand opening of West Shore Plaza from the September 27, 1967, edition of the *St Petersburg Independent*. The new mall featured air-conditioned comfort in an indoor setting with free parking, something downtown Tampa simply could not compete with. The two anchor stores were already operating when the mall opened. The first store to open was Maas Brothers on October 19, 1966, followed by J.C. Penney on September 7, 1967. The mall also featured a grocery store—Pantry Pride. Among the other new tenants were many well-known shops that left their landmark downtown locations, including Poller's Dress Shop, Lerner's Dress Shop, Bakers Shoes, and National Shirt Shops.

Four

YBOR CITY AND EAST TAMPA

Here is Ybor City's grand boulevard, Seventh Avenue, pictured in 1972 looking west from Eighteenth Street. Among the many stores and shops are the Latin American Furniture Store and Cuervo's Sandwich Shop. It is on this beloved street that generations of Tampa families and tourists have enjoyed shopping trips and dinner excursions. Much like Franklin Street in downtown Tampa, Seventh Avenue has always been the center of activity in Ybor City, Tampa's historic Latin Quarter. Tampa natives often refer to the street endearingly as La Septima; they know this is home to the best *café con leche* for dipping their Cuban toast in. During the glory years of the 1950s, all shopping was done here with many popular stores of that era lining both sides of the street, including Grant's, Woolworth's, Kress, J.C. Penney, and Belk-Lindsey. (*La Gaceta*.)

If there really was an Atlantis, Sebastian Agliano would have been mayor. In the early 1900s, Agliano rode a horse and buggy to Ybor City merchants delivering fresh seafood to local restaurants and cafés. In 1915, he founded his fish company at 1821 Seventh Avenue, pictured above in 1948. Sebastian and his wife, Rose, had seven children, and every one of them worked at the fish market and eventually had markets of their own. On Saturday mornings, the storefront was busy serving coffee and sandwiches to longtime customers who enjoyed sharing memories and talking politics with local politicians. In later years, Sebastian's grandson Buster Agliano took over the store and became an ardent civic leader and successful businessman. This was one of Ybor City's last family-owned businesses, which thrived for nearly 90 years and became one of the city's most legendary. The 1948 image below captures family and friends inside the store for a promotional advertisement.

This 1948 scene captures shoppers strolling along Seventh Avenue at the Fernandez and Garcia Department Store on the northeast corner of Seventh Avenue and Fifteenth Street in Ybor City. The store was opened by owners Juan Fernandez and Genaro Garcia, and Carolina Martinez was the luncheonette manager. (USFSCL.)

Poller's was one of the most recognizable names in ladies' wear during the 1940s, 1950s, and 1960s with locations in downtown and Ybor City. The location pictured here in 1940 was at 1623 Seventh Avenue. Poller's was a favorite dress shop for Tampa ladies and was operated by Nathan Poller. In later years, Poller's made their way into area shopping centers, including Northgate and Westshore Plaza. Next door is another shop using the 19th-century term *haberdashery* on its store sign.

Pictured here in 1935 is Tampa's oldest family-owned furniture store, Larmon's Furniture, in their landmark building at 1324 Seventh Avenue in Ybor City. The store was established in 1931 by business partners David Friday and Rubel Larmon. Rubel and his wife, Ermine, operated the store. In the above image, the couple's young sons Robert (left) and Curtis Larmon are standing at the store entrance. In later years, Curtis would take over the store from his father. The scene below captures a rare look inside the store in 1955. Of note is the advertised price of $299.95 for three rooms of new furniture.

Here are the Larmon boys Curtis (left) and Robert in their father's delivery truck, pictured in 1934. In 1955, Curtis Larmon partnered with his father, Rubel Larmon, to manage the store and later facilitated an expansion of the showroom from 4,000 to 20,000 square feet, allowing for a more diverse product line. The scene below from 1956 captures the store staff, including, from left to right, Rubel Larmon, Earl Johnson, Curtis Larmon, and Ermine Larmon. Four generations of the Larmon family have continued their legacy, and today, customers are welcomed by Elizabeth Larmon-Kalamaras and her husband, Jimmy Kalamaras, who operate the store.

This 1958 scene captures busy Seventh Avenue looking east from the corner of Fifteenth Street. The Ritz Theatre is pictured along with several stores and shops, including W.T. Grant's. The neon sign under the theater marquee advertises, "Air-Conditioned." During the 1950s, many Tampa residents experienced air-conditioning for the first time visiting area movie theaters. The theater and former W.T. Grant building pictured here are still standing today. In the image below from 1942 is Royal Jewelers at the southeast corner of Seventh Avenue and Fifteenth Street right next to the Ritz Theatre. (USFSCL.)

This nostalgic scene will certainly bring back memories for Ybor City residents who enjoyed shopping at S.H. Kress at 1624 East Seventh Avenue, pictured above in 1942. Notice the trademark red-and-gold sign that stretches across the entire storefront, commonly used by dime stores of this era. The storefront windows are filled with toys, cosmetics, dishes, and housewares. The sign reads, "5-10-25¢ store," another vintage remembrance of ages past. (*La Gaceta*.)

Here is the Miller's Outlet Store at 1515 East Seventh Avenue in 1950. The store sold women's clothing, gloves, hats, shoes, and accessories. The 1950 city directory listed Ethel H. Strauss as manager.

This is one of Ybor City's dime stores pictured in 1940 at 1600 Seventh Avenue. Of note is the nostalgic signage that advertised 5¢–10¢ across the storefront, very common with dime stores of this era. On display in the storefront windows at Silvers are an assortment of ladies' dresses, hats, linens, and fabrics.

This image captures Kinney's Shoe Store in 1936 at 1500 Seventh Avenue in Ybor City. The windows are filled with an assortment of shoes, and the advertised prices for a brand-new pair start at only $2.98. Of note are the vintage schoolhouse-type lights under the canopy. Kinney's Shoes was a popular store with another location in downtown on Franklin Street for many years.

Here is Ybor City's beloved W.T. Grant's Department Store at 1505 East Seventh Avenue in 1950. This was one of the largest stores along Seventh Avenue and a popular destination for Ybor City residents who shopped here for housewares, toys, books, records, clothing, linens, tools, lamps, school supplies, and other novelties. The scene below captures the store interior in 1950; toothpaste is advertised for 10¢ a tube, and ladies' perfume sets are on sale for 25¢.

Pictured here in 1940 is the Max Argintar menswear store at 1522 East Seventh Avenue in Ybor City. This store was a longtime favorite for gentlemen who could always find the finest in men's furnishings here, including suits, ties, hats, and gloves. The storefront windows are decorated with the latest in men's fashions of the 1940s.

Here is something never seen anymore: a family-owned neighborhood automotive parts store. This is Clark's Auto Supply, pictured in 1946 at 1402 Fourth Avenue in Ybor City, owned by Jesse H. Clark. The building is a classic American Art Deco design of the 1940s with large, rounded windows and glass-block entrance.

1921 – 1960

The Moré family has been operating bakeries for over 100 years. La Segunda Bakery's success story begins in 1907 when Juan Moré opened his first bakery at 1220 Seventh Avenue in Ybor City. The young baker fell in love with Cuban bread when he was serving in the Spanish-American War, so he decided to bring the Cuban delicacy to Tampa. In 1915, he opened his second bakery at 2512 Fifteenth Street, pictured above in 1921, appropriately naming it La Segunda (meaning "the second" in Spanish). Business flourished, and it became a neighborhood favorite. Four generations of the family have operated the bakery, producing 12,000 Cuban bread loaves daily for local and statewide delivery to restaurants, sandwich shops, and supermarkets. In the picture below, taken inside the bakery in 1980, Anthony Moré Jr. (left) stands with his father, Anthony Moré Sr., and little Copeland Moré, who manages the bakery today.

Oak Park Cleaners at 3210 East Seventh Avenue is pictured in 1950. At one time during the 1940s, this was Tampa's largest chain of dry cleaning stores with nearly 15 locations covering every neighborhood in the city and operating a large fleet of delivery trucks, several of which are parked under the canopy in this photograph. The Art Deco–style building still stands today as home to *La Gaceta*, the nation's only trilingual newspaper, now celebrating 90 years of service. The Manteiga family operates the newspaper, which is now a fourth-generation, family-operated business and a legendary Ybor City success story. (*La Gaceta*.)

Pictured here in 1956 is the Oak Park Sinclair gas station, and what a nostalgic scene has been captured. Located at the corner of Fiftieth Street and East Broadway, this classic gas station featured a dual-canopy design. The gas station attendant at left is wearing his 1950s-style uniform and cleaning the windshield for his customer. Notable are the vintage gas pumps and the whitewall tires on display outside the storefront window. Gas station attendants who would check oil and tires free of charge are another faded memory from ages past.

This photograph captures the J.B. Hardin Hardware Store at 2207 East Seventh Avenue in Ybor City in 1946. On display in the storefront windows is an assortment of 1950s-era toys, including a Radio Flyer wagon, a scooter, a pedal car, and bicycles. The store also sold farm supplies, tractors, tools, paint, and Goodyear tires. The business was owned by James and Daniel Wilbanks.

This 1951 photograph captures the Copeland's IGA Supermarket located at the corner of East Hillsborough Avenue and Thirtieth Street. The storefront window provides a rare glimpse into 1950s prices of the day, including the Super Suds laundry detergent for 19¢, bacon on sale for 35¢ per pound, Carnation canned milk at three for 39¢, Bisquick pancake mix for only 45¢, milk for just 29¢ per gallon, and toothpaste on sale at two for 19¢.

In October 1956, Justo "Bill" Noriega decided to open his drugstore in the one-stoplight town of Brandon, just east of Ybor City on Highway 60. The population of 2,000 was mostly farmers, and some of his first customers paid for their medicine with fresh eggs or bushels of fruit. The store now has three generations of family serving longtime customers. The store is pictured above in 1960 at the original location of 104 South Parsons Avenue. In 1972, Bill moved his wood-frame house and built his new larger store on that property at the corner of Carver Street and Highway 60 where it still stands today operated by his son and daughter John Noriega and Mary Noriega Denham. It is the oldest family-operated drugstore in Brandon. In the picture below, from 1976, John Noriega (left) stands with his father, Bill Noriega, outside the new store.

Pictured here in 1958 is Brandon Supply in their landmark building at the northeast corner of Highway 60 and Parsons Avenue. The store was founded in 1937 by brothers James and Jack Morgan, originally at the corner of Victoria Street and Parsons Avenue, north of the railroad crossing there. It was the only hardware store in this area of the county for many years. Local farmers and residents made this a regular stop every week for feed and grain, tools, hunting supplies, fishing supplies, lumber, paint, and garden supplies. The store also sold Hotpoint appliances. Of note are the vintage gasoline pumps near the store entrance. The store remained family owned for over 60 years.

The Shop-Rite Supermarket is pictured on grand opening day on March 31, 1958. This was one of Brandon's first large supermarkets and a welcome sight for residents living near the fast-developing Highway 60 corridor of the 1950s. The store was located near the corner of Highway 60 and Parsons Avenue.

The Scogin's Department Store success story beings in 1951 when I. Onie Scogin and his wife, Eunice Mae, built this little variety store at 305 East Highway 60 in the farming community of Brandon. This was the only 5-and-10 store in the entire area for many years, selling everything from kerosene to hamburgers. The family lived in a small area behind the store as they built up their business. The 1958 photograph below shows the expanded store completed after the highway was widened in the mid-1950s. The new, larger store offered an exclusive line of fine clothing for men, women, and children. This department store became a Brandon favorite where local residents shopped for many years before the arrival of shopping centers. The Scogin family continued to operate the store for over 40 years in this location, and the building still stands today as home to the Florida Orthopedic Institute.

Five

Palma Ceia and
South Tampa

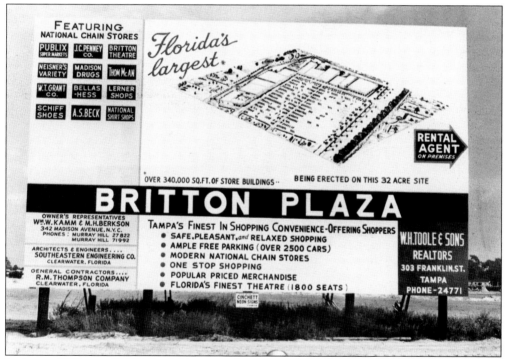

In August 1956, over 25,000 South Tampa residents arrived at the grand opening of its first shopping center, and Britton Plaza opened with much fanfare and a carnival in the parking lot. The rapid population growth in South Tampa during the 1950s shifted shopping from the exclusivity of downtown into neighborhood shopping centers, and Britton Plaza was the king of them all. The 1956 picture above captures the billboard announcing plans for the 32-acre site with 38 stores planned and a new 1,800-seat theater, considered the largest in the state at that time. It was a new concept in shopping for the city and one that would eventually change the dynamics of Tampa's retail industry forever. The massive complex was constructed by the R.M. Thompson Company and designed by Southeastern Engineering Company, both of Clearwater, Florida.

Here is the Eggner-Diaz men's shop at Britton Plaza in 1956. Hollis Eggner partnered with Armando Diaz to open his first store at 208 Zack Street in 1952. Eggner began working at the Wolf Brothers menswear store in 1934, making deliveries when he was 14 years old, and continued working there for 18 years. With his savvy administrative experience and fashion-designing skills perfected, he ran his own chain of local stores for nearly 20 years and became a local favorite for Tampa gentlemen with a discerning taste in fine clothing. At one time, Eggner-Diaz had five locations, including stores in Tampa, Largo, and Lake Wales.

Many Tampa residents will remember going to Western Auto for their first bicycle. Pictured in 1956 is the location at 1100 South Dale Mabry Highway in Palma Ceia. The store is celebrating summer with a boat show, and there are several 1950s-style speedboats and fishing boats on display for the crowd to enjoy. Next door is the A&P Supermarket.

This Britton Plaza music shop pictured in 1956 certainly evokes nostalgic memories. In the storefront window are quite an assortment of 1950s-style record players, hi-fi systems, tabletop radios, and floor-model radios. The Gourlie Music Company also sold musical instruments and certainly must have seen many students from nearby high schools, like Plant and Robinson, coming in to select their favorite band instruments and pick out a record on the way home. This music company had a very long history of success in Tampa.

This Table Supply Supermarket was at 1407 South Howard Avenue in 1948. Advertised prices include bacon for 59¢ per pound and canned peas for two for 35¢.

The success story of State Vacuum begins in 1947 at the original location in the 1600 block of Grand Central Avenue (now Kennedy Boulevard), pictured above around 1952. The store's lead salesman was a young Bernie Epstein, who broke all sales records in company history and became a national trainer for the sales force. Bernie advanced up the ranks in the company, and he purchased the store in 1959, renamed it State Vacuum of Tampa, and began his mission to make his store Tampa's leading vacuum cleaner dealer. Pictured below in 1967 is company founder Bernie Epstein inside the store. On the back wall, several vintage, mid-century-styled canister vacuum cleaners are displayed.

By 1965, Bernie Epstein had outgrown his small storefront and wanted to expand his product line, so he purchased a former Gulf gas station at 3123 Kennedy Boulevard. The gas station was modified into a retail showroom and office, pictured above in 1967. Eventually, Bernie would enlarge the store to more than 20,000 square feet of showroom space, calling it "The World's Largest Vacuum Cleaner Store." Pictured below in 1972 is David Epstein (left) with his father, Bernie Epstein, inside the store. David continues his family legacy of personalized customer service today and has a loyal following of longtime Tampa customers, making it Tampa's premier vacuum cleaner store.

Here are two storefronts in the Carriage Trade Plaza at 1718 South Dale Mabry Highway in 1958. During the 1950s, this area between Henderson Boulevard and Bay to Bay Boulevard became a popular retail corridor with small shopping plazas, cafés, and stores lining both sides of the street. Pictured here are Fleischman's Kiddie Shoppe, which specialized in children's clothing, and the Revere McLoud Millinery, which specialized in ladies' hats and lingerie. Their sign uses the 19th-century term *millinery*. This shopping center still stands today and is still home to many family-owned businesses.

Pictured here in 1968 is the Simon Schwartz Supermarket, which opened in 1950 at 404 South MacDill Avenue. The Schwartz family has a long history in the market business dating back to the early 1900s when H.W. Schwartz operated his store in Ybor City. The Schwartz family markets always provided their customers with specialized service and happily fulfilled special requests. Many South Tampa families frequented this store for over 40 years; shoppers always got top-notch meats and specialty items not found elsewhere.

Here is the Lil' General Store at 3342 South Westshore Boulevard in 1959. There are many interesting nostalgic symbols to enjoy, including the elaborate neon sign and the advertisement below it with one gallon of milk on sale for 79¢. The storefront featured an open-air design for neighborhood residents to walk into, and overhead garage doors were pulled down at closing time. Of note are the vintage telephone booth and the monument-style concrete street marker next to the sign.

Lazzara's Market, pictured at right in 1968, was a neighborhood favorite located at 1109 Swann Avenue in Hyde Park. The market opened in 1945 and was family operated by Sam and Mary Lazzara for over 30 years. South Tampa residents fondly remember the fresh produce and flowers lining the sidewalks in front of the store, which was also a popular stop for nearby attorneys and doctors on their way home from work.

In 1947, Arthur Yates took his first job as a jeweler at the Alan Doss Jewelry Store in his hometown of Plant City, Florida. Soon after, Yates became a skilled watch repairman at the Hayman Jewelry Company in downtown Tampa, but he really wanted to open his own store. In 1950, Arthur Yates realized his dream and opened his first jewelry store in a small building at 3636 Henderson Boulevard in South Tampa. Pictured below is an antique car that was parked out front as his store signage, a clever advertising gimmick he used to attract new customers. The above photograph was taken in 1967 at the opening of the new, expanded store at 3802 Neptune Street.

In the 1967 photograph above, Arthur Yates and his wife, Betty, are celebrating the grand opening of their new large store at 3802 Neptune Street near the busy Dale Mabry Highway retail corridor in Palma Ceia. In the 1947 photograph below, Arthur Yates can be seen working on watch repairs at the Alan Doss Jewelry Store in Plant City, Florida, where he started his career in the jewelry industry. Today, the family-owned store continues its tradition of friendly, personalized service with Arthur Yates's sons David and Ron running the store, now located at 1708 South Dale Mabry Highway.

The Lang family was well known for the success of their local ice cream shops during the 1940s and 1950s. In 1957, the family went from dipping ice cream cones to dipping into the pool business with Lang Aquatech Pools, their new pool company on South Dale Mabry Highway pictured here. Robert Stewart Lang became Tampa's most well-known pool man, building nearly 10,000 pools statewide for homeowners, motels, hotels, and municipalities. He also was an innovative pool designer nationally recognized for his expertise in the advancement of safety features for pool construction. In the picture below from the store's grand opening in 1957 is the innovative concept of the take-home pool in a box.

These 1952 photographs capture the grand opening of the Peninsula Appliance store at 2101 South Dale Mabry Highway. The store specialized in Crosley appliances, internationally known for their fine radios. Looking inside the store below provides a rare glimpse of 1950s-era appliances and televisions, including several vintage washing machines and kitchen stoves. The store was operated by Paul Antinori when this photograph was taken.

Here is the Galloway's Furniture Store at 3347 Henderson Boulevard, pictured in 1957. Established by Ralph Galloway in 1948, this store was one of the city's most well known, supplying young Tampa couples with the furniture for their first homes during the city's population boom of the 1950s. The family-owned store thrived for nearly 60 years and became an icon in South Tampa, known for its expansive selection of contemporary furniture. Over the decades, the store sold furniture to thousands of customers, many of whom remained loyal through various decor trends. The store closed in October 2007.

Pictured here in 1957 is the Morton-Williams Clothing Store at 1707 South Dale Mabry Highway in South Tampa. Morton-Williams sold clothing and shoes at their downtown store for many years and decided to move into the expanding Dale Mabry Highway retail corridor during the 1950s. The store was operated by J. Morton Williams, Edward Williams, and Amelia Williams.

The Sellers family has been in the camera business for over 60 years. In 1953, a young, 20-year-old Sam Sellers opened his third photograph shop, pictured here in 1966 at 6832 South MacDill Avenue. Sam was working as the official photographer for MacDill Air Force Base with assignments that included top-secret military aircraft and promotional photographs for commanders. He perfected his skills with training from an elite team of military photographers. In later years, Sam expanded to five locations in Tampa with each of his three children operating a store. His son Sam Sellers Jr. continues the family legacy today, operating the Golden Triangle Photo Shop on Kennedy Boulevard in South Tampa.

Pictured in 1951 is the Military Exchange Company located at 6815 South MacDill Avenue just a few blocks north of MacDill Air Force Base. This business owner was smart to select a location offering uniforms, fatigues, helmets, boots, and other military-type clothing to the young officers living nearby. The store was operated by I. Ray Schneider.

Pictured in 1959, Kirby's Menswear is a well-known South Tampa fixture with a historic past. The Shine family has an enduring legacy that dates back to 1911 when Louis Shine opened the Palace, his Ybor City store on Seventh Avenue. In 1945, Louis's son Mark Shine married department store royalty Audrey Maas, and she proved to be his good luck charm working alongside him at his father's store. In 1959, Mark chose a developing area of Dale Mabry Highway to open his new store specializing in fine menswear and supplying South Tampa businessmen with an extensive selection of tailored suits and accessories. Today, his son Martin Shine continues the family tradition as owner of the third-generation, family-operated store located at 1707 South Dale Mabry Highway. In the 1970 photograph below, Mark Shine (left) coordinates a clothing drive at the store to benefit Goodwill Industries.

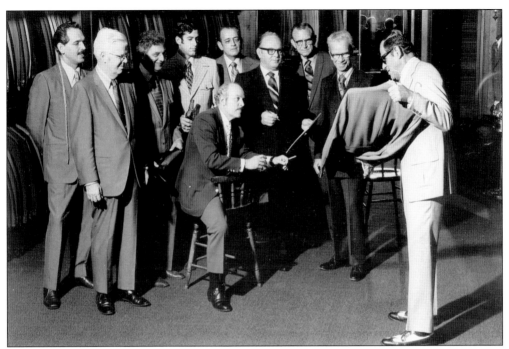

In this 1970 photograph taken inside Kirby's Menswear, Mark Shine is leading a sales meeting with employees. Pictured are, from left to right, (first row) Engle Becraft, Joe Alvarez, Walter Diaz, Phil McGuire and Mark Shine; (second row) Rudy Antinori, Nyman Elias, Stephen Shine, John Scolaro, and Britt Ware.

In this 1975 photograph, Mark Shine's son Stephen Shine is posing outside the South Dale Mabry Highway storefront wearing the latest fashion trends in 1970s menswear. Stephen also works at the store today along with his mother, Audrey Maas-Shine, carrying on that trademark, personalized, friendly service in memory of their beloved patriarch, Mark Shine. The store has offered fine menswear to South Tampa gentlemen for over 50 years.

Here is Chan's Toy Shop in 1956, located at 4107 Henderson Boulevard near Dale Mabry Highway in South Tampa with its unique neon sign on the roof—a stack of baby blocks. This store was one of the city's most popular where neighborhood children gathered to enjoy the slot car track races and pick out their first bicycles. This is where collections started for Matchbox cars, Barbie dolls, toy soldiers, model airplanes, radio kits, and dollhouses. Notable is the stack of Radio Flyer wagons on display outside for children of all ages. The store was owned by George Chandler.

Here is the Gandy Liquors store at 3103 West Gandy Boulevard, pictured in 1954. The building is a classic 1950s-style design, and the neon sign is an elaborate piece of flashy artwork with a giant neon bottle popping the cork to draw the attention of drivers passing by.

V.T. Clark's Market has been a Port Tampa fixture for over 50 years in this redbrick landmark building at the southeast corner of Westshore and Interbay Boulevards, pictured above in 1950. In 1960, V.T. Clark and his wife, Margaret, bought the building and opened their store. In later years, the entire family would help run the store, including their daughter Sue Clark-Scott and her husband, Loren Scott, who still operates the store today. The building was originally constructed in 1920 by local contractor H.J. Hanks, who named it "Hank's Corner," and it became home to many different stores over the years, including Kelton's Drugstore and Law's Grocery Store. V.T. Clark's was the only variety store in the area for many years, offering everything from kerosene to fresh meats. Handbills advertising the store's sale prices were distributed door to door on Saturdays by neighborhood children who often would take the homeowners' shopping list back to the store for delivery later.

This little family-owned drugstore was located at 3910 South MacDill Avenue in 1950. The signs all use the 19th-century term *sundries*. The store also offered "fountain service," another mid-century nostalgic term for the offering of ice cream sodas and milk shakes inside the store, all hand-dipped at the counter.

Shoppers here at Sumner's Food Market were welcomed by William and Margaret Sumner. The Sumner family operated several supermarkets around the city during the 1940s and 1950s. The store pictured here in 1956 was at 2815 South MacDill Avenue, and this building still stands today, home to the Salvation Army Thrift Store.

This family-owned Firestone Tire store was located at 2819 South MacDill Avenue in 1948. Many Firestone stores also sold appliances and sporting goods in their early days. The neon sign on the storefront proudly features the name of owner Warner Grable. The building still stands today, home to a Beef O' Brady's restaurant.

Three generations of the Tarr family have been in the Tampa furniture market dating back to 1904 with the establishment of the Tarr Furniture Company. Russell H. Tarr was a pioneer in the industry with a seven-story furniture store considered to be one of the finest in the Southeast, still standing today at the corner of Lafayette Street and Hyde Park Avenue. The store pictured here in 1959 was a South Tampa favorite at 3410 Henderson Boulevard, and the family tradition continues today with Ginger Tarr Shea operating her interior design company in Hyde Park.

Pictured here in 1958 is the Record City record shop at 1531 South Dale Mabry Highway. This was a popular after-school hangout for students from nearby Plant High School, who will remember stopping here on the way home to pick up the latest releases from those great 1950s-era rock-and-roll legends. Of note is the flashy, 1950s, musically inspired neon sign.

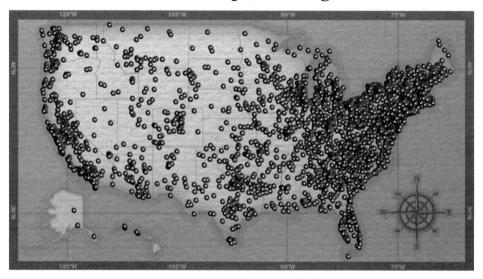